D0817130

FRIENDS
for Life

A Thank-You for a Friend
Who's Been There
Through the Years

Edited by Sarah Wilson

Blue Mountain Press™
Boulder, Colorado

We wish to thank Susan Polis Schutz for permission to reprint the following poems that appear in this publication: "We're Lifetime Friends," "Some people will be your friend...," "Our Friendship Will Endure," "I Don't Know What I'd Do Without You," and "I Am So Lucky to Have You as a Friend." Copyright © 1982, 1986, 1987, 1988 by Stephen Schutz and Susan Polis Schutz. All rights reserved.

Library of Congress Control Number: 2011961147
ISBN: 978-1-59842-641-0

◪ and Blue Mountain Press are registered in U.S. Patent and Trademark Office. Certain trademarks are used under license.

Printed in China.
Second Printing: 2012

✪ This book is printed on recycled paper.

This book is printed on paper that has been specially produced to be acid free (neutral pH) and contains no groundwood or unbleached pulp. It conforms with the requirements of the American National Standards Institute, Inc., so as to ensure that this book will last and be enjoyed by future generations.

Blue Mountain Arts, Inc.

P.O. Box 4549, Boulder, Colorado 80306

Contents

Friends for Life

One of the nicest things in my entire life is having a friend like you. It is a privilege to have you here sharing our time together.

You understand so much, so naturally, and I rely on you to help me keep my feet on the ground, my dreams on the horizon, my hopes in my heart, and my faith in tomorrow. And you never let me down.

I think you are unaware of how extraordinary you are and how beautiful you will always be. But I just want you to know... you have never been anything less than amazing to me.

— Sandy Jamison

I Wouldn't Trade My Friendship with You for Anything

One of the best feelings
in the whole world
comes from being a friend
and having a friend in return.

I wouldn't trade my friendship
with you for anything... because I know
that nothing else could ever begin
to bring me the contentment,
the wonderful craziness,
the support and the caring,
the laughter, the understanding,
and all the thousands of things
that we experience together.

One of the sweetest feelings
in the whole world
comes from knowing that
everything we share — and the joy
that graces our lives — will warm our
hearts forever, in all the days ahead.

For no matter how far apart
our paths may wander
and no matter how long it's been,
it's so great to know that...

you and I will always be
   the closest and dearest
      of friends.

— Lorrie Westfall

We Are
Kindred Spirits

Every so often,
fate brings two souls together —
kindred spirits whose paths
have crossed in another life...
and there is never a disconnect.

We don't have to talk every day to know
the other is only a phone call away.
It's just a fact: we would drop everything
for each other if needed.

Yet when we do connect,
we pick up right where we left off.
Our conversations begin and end mid-paragraph.
We both know where to start up again —
like we were never apart.

What a comfort it is to have you in my life!
A wonderful blessing...
a fabulous friend.
Kindred spirits...
kindred souls.

— Suzy Toronto

Forever Friendship

Sometimes in life,
you find a special friend:
someone who makes you laugh
until you can't stop;
someone who makes you believe
that there really is good in the world;
someone who convinces you
that there is an unlocked door
just waiting for you to open it.
This is forever friendship.

When you're down
and the world seems dark and empty,
your forever friend lifts you up in spirit
and makes that dark and empty world
suddenly seem bright and full.

Your forever friend gets you through
the hard times, the sad times,
and the confused times.
If you turn and walk away,
your forever friend follows.
If you lose your way,
your forever friend guides you
and cheers you on.
Your forever friend holds your hand
and tells you that
everything is going to be okay.
And if you find such a friend,
you feel happy and complete
because you need not worry.
You have a forever friend for life,
and forever has no end.

— Laurieann Kelly

In a lifetime,
you get only a few lifelong friends.
And when you find them,
you always know them
by sight and heart alone.
And when you find them,
you always grow a little bit
taller in your soul.
And when you find them,
you also know that
as the years come and
as the years go by,
you have been blessed
just to know them.
Thus blessed am I,
thus lucky have I been
to know a friend like you.

— Ashley Rice

From the Beginning, I Knew Our Friendship Was Unique

I remember when we first became friends
and how wonderful it felt
as our friendship deepened over time.
We both discovered that
we could tell each other anything
and know we would find
compassion and acceptance.
I'm grateful for each time
you were there when I needed you,
and I am deeply thankful for
the kindness you've given so freely.

I've called on you in some of

the darkest and brightest times in my life.

I've revealed my fears and heartaches to you,

and you've given me the strength to bear them.

I've shared my hopes

and hard—won achievements with you,

and in you I found someone who

believed in me all along.

No matter how much time passes,

please know I always appreciate you.

Your friendship is a gift beyond measure.

— Susan Shone

Some Things Never Change

If our friendship has changed at all through the years, it has just gotten better with time. We may not know all the reasons we came into each other's life and stayed, but I like to think that God has angels assigned to finding His children good friends. I guess a skeptic would say that our friendship is just a coincidence; I don't know. But what's important is we're still here on this planet together and happy that we're in each other's life. I guess it really doesn't matter what the reason is. I'm just thankful it's true — that we're still friends after all these years.

— Donna Fargo

Friendship Is...

Friendship is such a remarkable thing ◆ Friendship is two people who totally understand each other ◆ Friendship is so powerful ◆ It gives you support and strength to see your way through ◆ Friendship is a helping hand from someone with a very big heart ◆ If there is a wall of worry in your life, a friend will help you get over it ◆ Friendship is acceptance in its most beautiful form ◆ It is filled with grins and taking you in and giving you the kind of hugs that warm your whole world ◆

Friendship is a talking, listening, trusting thing ➤ It reminds you that you don't have to keep everything bottled up inside ➤ It lets the genie out and helps so many wishes come true ➤ Friendship is the lovely reassurance of knowing that someone will always be there to check in on you ➤ Friendship is tons of fun, completely sweet, and enormously wonderful ➤

You never know where life is going to take you, but if you've got a friend to share the journey with... you've already been blessed with one of the most priceless gifts there is ➤

— Douglas Pagels

I Am So Lucky to
Have You as
a Friend

Sometimes we are lucky enough
to meet a person
who stands out
among all the other people
as being extremely special
who knows what we
are thinking about
who is happy for us at all times
who is always there to talk to us
who cares about us selflessly
who is always truthful with us
Sometimes we are lucky enough
to meet someone who is
extremely wonderful
For me
that person
is you
my dear friend

— Susan Polis Schutz

What a Friend Does

A friend will be there
when you really need someone
and will come to you
when they need help.
A friend will listen to you
even when they don't understand
or agree with your feelings;
a friend will never try to change you
but appreciates you for who you are.
A friend doesn't expect too much
or give too little;
a friend is someone you can share
dreams, hopes, and feelings with.
A friend is a person you can think of
and suddenly smile;
a friend doesn't have to be told
that they are special,
because they know you feel that way.

A friend will accept your attitudes,
ideas, and emotions,
even when their own are different;
a friend will hold your hand
when you're scared.
A friend will be honest with you,
even when it might hurt,
and will forgive you for your mistakes.
A friend can never disappoint you
and will support you
and share in your glory.
A friend shares responsibility
when you have doubts.
A friend always remembers
the little things you've done,
the times you've shared,
and the talks you've had.
A friend will bend over backward
to help you pick up the pieces
when your world falls apart.
A friend is one of life's most beautiful gifts.

— Luann Auciello

You Are
an Inspiration

I see your gifts reflected in others.
I watch them savor your smiling eyes.
I watch them brighten up when you shower them
with your spontaneous laughter.
I watch them when you look into their eyes
and ask them how they are doing —
they can tell you really want to know.
These are the moments they remember
at the end of their day.

You have the gift of giving and the gift of receiving.
You accept the quiet "thank you"
whispered in gratitude,
the glimpse of a happy tear,
and the face beaming love back to you.
You allow others to slip into your heart
and energize your soul.
You return that love to them joyfully.

You make a difference in others' lives,
and you allow them to make a difference in yours.

— Susan L. Roberts

Sometimes I find myself thinking of you — of your strength and motivation and the amazing way you manage to keep it all together. I see how others look at you, and I know that they think these same things about you too. For as many times as these thoughts surround you, I hope you know how truly wonderful you are and how much you are admired by those who are lucky enough to be a part of your life.

— Elle Mastro

You are appreciated
and praised quite often
by a lot of people in your life
for your helpful ways and caring heart.
And though I'm sure
you don't see yourself as someone special,
I want you to know that you are.

There aren't many people I know
who reach out to others in need
even when they have
a busy life like you do.
There aren't many people
who are so delighted
to care for others the way you do.

So many people celebrate
the ways you touch their lives —
and I hope you believe me,
because I'm one of them!

— Dianne Cogar

I Admire
So Much
About You

I admire the life that you lead
and the kindness that is such a sweet
and natural part of you.

I admire the way you treat other people.

I admire how easily a smile finds its way
to your face.

I admire the work that you do
and the places your journeys take you.

I admire your dedication
to all the right things and your devotion
to your friends and your family.

I admire how completely you care
and how willingly you are always there
for the people who need you.

I admire you with all my heart
for being the light that you are to my life.

— L. N. Mallory

You aren't just an ordinary person.
You are a person who is unique and special
and who fits into my life perfectly.

It doesn't matter what I'm doing
or what I am thinking about...

When you come to mind, a warmth steals
into my heart and a smile comes to my lips.
And I think about how lucky I am to know you.

— Barbara Cage

I have always felt like
I can count on you for anything
and I would never be let down.
You go out of your way
to make my life happier,
and the little things you do
mean so very much to me.
You have such a big heart
filled with so much kindness and love.
I feel so very blessed to have you in my life.

— Elle Mastro

You're My Every-Day-Angel

Not all angels have wings.

But they're angels all the same.

You can tell them from the smiles they inspire, the hugs they give, and the way they bless other people's lives with so much abundance.

You are an every-day-angel to me, a truly beautiful one, and I don't know what I'd ever do without you.

I am beyond lucky to have you in my life.

I don't have all the words to express how important you are to me. Some words just don't go deep enough. But I want to say a very special thanks all the same. And...

I hope you know how much you're loved.

— Lorrie Westfall

Sweet Offering

"Is there anything I can do?"
You've asked me
    that sweet question
        many times over the years.

Your heart,
your mind,
your schedule,
your home,
your pocketbook
    are always open to me
        if I need them.

Sometimes there's nothing
you can do...
    and we both know it.

But still you offer.
And in your offering
    I find everything I need.

        — BJ Gallagher

People like you
make the world a better place,
because you think of ways
to make a positive difference
in the lives of others.

People like you
make those you come in contact with
feel special by acts of kindness
and deeds of thoughtfulness.

People like you
deserve the best out of life,
because that's what you give.

— Barbara Cage

Friends are very special people who accept
each other with an unconditional caring. They

Recognize each other's talents and faults and
acknowledge them without judgment.

They are Incapable of turning away when times
are tough and life's problems seem hard to bear.

Instead, they Encourage each other so they can
enjoy the good times and find strength to endure the

bad times. They're Never afraid to say what
they feel and can be honest without causing

hurt or pain. They can Depend on each other
because they have the kind of trust

that allows them to Share the best and worst
of their lives with laughter and without fear.

— Andrea L. Hines

You Are a Real Friend

When two people are real friends, they both know it in their hearts. They don't have to question whether or not they have a friendship. They're at the top of each other's list when they want to share something good or not so good in their lives. They offer their help before even being asked. They're the first to hear complaints and problems, and they give each other perspective and support. Trust and freedom come with friendship, and real friends value these blessings.

We all appreciate our acquaintances and value our relationships, but real friends are treasures in each other's heart. They show up when others don't. They think about each other and show their feelings, not only by what they say, but also by what they do for each other. They talk freely and don't have to guard their words. They believe in each other and know they will be there for whatever they're each having to face in life. They are real friends, like you.

— Donna Fargo

Some people will be your friend
because of whom you know
Some people will be your friend
because of your position
Some people will be your friend
because of the way you look
Some people will be your friend
because of your possessions
But the only real friends
are the people who will be your friends
because they like you for how you are inside
That is the true meaning of friendship
I want to thank you for being
one of the very few people in my life
who is a real friend
— Susan Polis Schutz

You Are My Best Friend

You are the one person
who shares my deepest thoughts
and loves me in spite of them.
You counsel me when my heart is broken,
and you stand by me when I'm mistreated.
You rally behind me in my good decisions
and are there to help me through
the consequences of the bad ones.
Who else can I call at any hour of the day or night?
Who else accepts and understands all of me?
Not many people are as blessed as I am
with someone like you in their lives.

I don't know why the heavens decided to give me
the wonderful gift of you as my friend,
but I'm grateful.
No matter what comes along, good or bad,
it brings me great comfort and security
to know that I can always count on you.
I hope you know in your heart that
I am that same sort of friend to you.
Our secrets are safe and our hearts are protected
because of the love between us...
two special friends.

— Pamela Malone–Melton

We Make a Great Team

Our hearts are interlocked,
and what we are together
makes us stronger
and helps us persevere.
Together we've tried our wings;
we've soared high and crashed,
celebrated and cried.
We've dried each other's tears
and picked up the pieces
of broken dreams.

Together we've made things
better than they were before.
It's not even so much the help
we've given each other;
it's the absolute confidence
that we're always there —
wanting, willing, and ready to help.

— Vickie M. Worsham

Through the Years, You Have Been Such a Good Friend

We have all had many friends
throughout our lives,
but only a few of them
we would call good friends.
That's because being a good friend
involves time and understanding and love,
which can be difficult to share with another.

When I think of my good friends,
I always think about you,
because that is what you have been to me.
You have taken the time
to be there when I needed you,
and you have listened to me
when my life was changing.

You have always cared enough
to try to understand my feelings
and help me to understand myself.
And, most importantly,
your consideration and honesty
have shown me
that your friendship is true...
symbolizing a very special kind of love
that only a few friends
ever share with one another.

— Laura Medley

I Don't Know
What I'd Do
Without You

It is easy to find a friend
when things are going well
and everyone can have fun together

It is easy to find a friend
when exciting things are happening
and everyone can look forward to them together

It is easy to find a friend
when the environment is attractive
and everyone can be happy together

But the friend that we find
who will be with us
when we are having problems
and our lives are confused
is a hard friend to find

Thank you for being
one of those rare people
who is a
real friend
for life

— Susan Polis Schutz

I'll Always Be There for You

When there are clouds in your sky...

If you have stuff you want to bounce off someone, I'll listen. If you want to cry, I'll do what I can to help you dry your tears. When you need to be alone, I'll give you your space, but I'll also walk with you through the storms if you want me to. If you're down, I'll encourage you and we'll chase hope and laughter till we catch them.

And when there is sunshine in your life...

If you want someone to celebrate with, I'll be happy for you. If you need to brag a bit about yourself, that's okay too. When you're on cloud nine, I'll be there with you to soak up the sun and share your joy. If you want someone just to have fun and enjoy the day with, I'm ready.

Through the sunshine and the clouds, during the highs, the lows, and all the in-betweens, I'll always be there for you.

— Donna Fargo

What I See
in You

I'm sure you already know
   just how special you are,
and I'm sure you can see that you make
a big difference in the lives of those around you,
but it just feels really good
   to remind you sometimes
that my own life wouldn't be as wonderful
   as it is without you in it too.

In you, I see a giver, a helper,
   and a supporter.
In you, I see a peacemaker,
   a strong shoulder to lean on,
      and a loyal friend.
But even all these things don't say enough
   about the wonderful person you are.

Even though you already know this,
   I want to say it anyway.
You are one terrific person.
                    — Dianne Cogar

You Are the Beautiful Flower in My Life

Over the years, one begins to have a clear understanding of what a friend is. True friends do not come into your life every day, but they do come. No matter the length of time they are physically with us, they eternally remain in our hearts — that specific place of memory and meeting.

A friend can quiet a fear, help you keep your perspective, and show you there is always room for humor. A friend shares your joy or sadness, regardless of what is going on in her own life. A friend gives you advice when there's some to give, remains quiet when there's none, and knows the difference between the two.

A friend listens to you talk about a problem for the hundredth time without rolling her eyes; she knows you will find the answer one day.

A friend keeps faith for you when yours is dwindling and keeps confidence in you until yours is restored. A friend says with strong resolve "It will come," "Things will work out," or "Keep following your heart," and you trust what she says because the conviction in her voice and something in your heart tell you that you can.

Above all, a friend is like a beautiful flower: unique in its bloom, distinct from any other, adding merit and grace to your life.

— Marianne Coyne

Special people are those who have the ability to share their lives with others. They are honest in word and deed, they are sincere and compassionate, and they always make sure that love is a part of everything.

Special people are those who have the ability to give to others and help them with the changes that come their way. They are not afraid of being vulnerable; they believe in their uniqueness and are proud to be who they are.

Special people are those who allow themselves the pleasures of being close to others and caring about their happiness. They have come to understand that love is what makes the difference in life.

You are a very, very special person who truly makes a beautiful difference in this world.

— Deanna Beisser

True Friendship Has Many Ingredients

True friendship isn't seen
with the eyes;
it's felt with the heart
when there is trust,
understanding, secrets,
loyalty, and sharing.

Friendship is a feeling
rarely found in life,
but when it is found,
it has a profound impact
on one's well-being,
strength, and character.
A true friendship does not need
elaborate gifts or spectacular events
in order to be valuable or valued.

To ensure long-lasting quality
and satisfaction,
a friendship only needs
certain key ingredients:
undying loyalty,
unmatched understanding,
unsurpassed trust,
deep and soulful secrets,
and endless sharing.
These ingredients, mixed with
personality and a sense of humor,
can make friendship
last a lifetime.

— Sonya Williams

Lifelong Friends
Are like the Stars

Distance may separate us,
but friends are always there to
shine upon our triumphs,
guide us through darkness,
and show us we are never alone.
Lifelong friends give beauty to our lives,
inspiration to our souls, and
peace to our hearts.

— Katie Newell

Our Friendship Will Endure

Friends always remember so well
all the things they did together
all the subjects they discussed
all the mistakes they made
all the fun they had
Friends always remember
how their friendship
was such a stabilizing force
during confusing times
in their lives

Friends may have different lifestyles
live in different places
and interact with different people
but no matter how much
their lives may change
their friendship remains the same
I know that throughout my life
wherever I am
I will always
remember so well
and cherish our friendship
as one of the best
I have ever known

— Susan Polis Schutz

Thank you...

For keeping my spirits up.

For never letting me down.

For being here for me.

For knowing I'm there for you.

For bringing so many smiles my way.

For being sensitive to my needs.

For knowing just what to say.

For listening better than anyone else.

For bringing me laughter.

For bringing me light.

For understanding so much about me.

For trusting me with so much about you.

For being the best.

For being so beautiful.

I don't know what I'd do without you.

— Collin McCarty

When I'm with You, Everything Is Better

There's a big difference between spending time with most people in life... and spending time with a friend. Many people barely connect; the rush-about world doesn't allow for much of an opportunity to move beyond the surface sort of interaction or the simple sharing of minutes in the day.

But when I'm with you, everything is different. The world slows down. The sun comes out. Things that haven't seen the light of day in a while suddenly become clearer and brighter. Things are so much nicer. Words come easily, freely, truthfully.

Because our friendship is so important to me, our times together take on so much significance. When I'm with you, a little walk can turn into an adventure, a brief conversation can capture absolutely everything that's on our minds, and our minutes can turn into moments... that mean the world to me.

There is a foundation we've built, and it's solid and certain and more reassuring than my words can begin to say. There's the sweet feeling that we can spend the day doing everything or nothing at all... and that regardless of what we choose to do, we will have a better time than anyone could ever imagine.

Together, without even trying to, you and I always manage to make the most of the moments we're given. And in so doing, I think we add a tremendous amount of meaning and comfort and wonder to the moments we have... and to the lives we are living.

— Douglas Pagels

I'd Love to
Give You
These Gifts...

Joy that shines on you along every path you walk

Faith to guide you so you never feel lost

Hope to keep you positive and strong

Peace — so you can hear the songs

    that sing in your heart

Sunshine to dry any tears

Childlike wonder to have and hold

    in your eyes, heart, and soul

A wealth of good friends to show you and tell you

    how much you mean to the world

Simple pleasures to celebrate and remember

Energy to leap for your highest dreams

Confidence in your talents and your power

    to attract success

Courage to stick to your principles

Respect for your feelings, needs, and dreams

Laughter wherever your spirit travels

Family connections that nurture, protect, encourage,

    and help you flourish as an individual

Adventures that widen your horizons

Love that comes with all these other wishes

    that are in my heart for you

— Jacqueline Schiff

There Is No Stronger Bond Than Friendship

Friendship is about two people caring for each other just the way they are. It's about appreciating another person and sharing the everyday stuff of life.

Friendship is about being supportive all the time — not just when it's convenient. It's about prayers and hopes for someone who's a big part of your life. It's about having someone on your side who not only hears but listens — and who not only talks the talk but walks the walk.

It's about having a special person in your life who truly wants the best for you — and who proves it time and again by words and actions that instill confidence and trust.

Friendship is knowing that you have someone who will be there — not only when nothing much is making sense, but also when you're sailing free and easy toward the top.

Friendship is that unwritten exchange of loyalty with a person who knows you inside out. It's the gift that keeps on giving and the treasure we'll never lose. It's about you and me and the bond that tells us both we're not in this alone.

— Donna Fargo

We're Lifetime Friends

Though we don't see each other very much
nor do we write to each other very much
nor do we phone each other very much
I always know that, at any time
I could call, write or see you
and everything would be exactly the same
You would understand everything I am saying
and everything that I am thinking

Our friendship does not depend
on being together
It is deeper than that
Our closeness is something inside of us
that is always there
ready to be shared with each other
whenever the need arises

It is such a comfortable and warm feeling
to know that
we have such a lifetime
friendship

— Susan Polis Schutz

Old Friends Are the Most Cherished Ones

There is nothing like an old friend.
With old friends, the only requirement
is that you be yourself.
You can say whatever is on your mind
and do whatever you feel like doing.
You never have to worry, because
you know your friendship is not based
on perfection, but on respect
and acceptance.

With old friends,
you can share the most intimate
and important aspects of yourself,
knowing that their beauty and value
will be recognized and appreciated.

With old friends,
distance has no meaning or power.
There's a bridge made of
love and memories,
joys and sorrows,
that connects old friends
and keeps them close.

With old friends, you feel safe.
They've been there for you
through the roughest storms,
so you know you can trust them,
believe in them, and count on them.
You know they will be at your side,
so there is peace within your heart.

With old friends, you never feel lonely,
because the roots that bind you
have grown deep and strong.
Your friendship has withstood
the test of time.

— Nancye Sims

Friendship Is Traveling the Same Path Together

Friendship is opening up to one another. It's sharing thoughts and feelings in a way that never felt very comfortable before. It is a complete trust, sweetened with a lot more understanding and communication than many people will ever know.

Friendship is two hearts that share and that are able to say things no outsiders ever could. Friendship is an inner door that only a friend has the key to. Friendship is a gift, continually giving happiness. It is strong and supportive, and few things in all the world will ever compare with the joy that comes from its wonderful bond.

— Mia Evans

Friends Are the Best Gifts of All

Friends are the people who encourage you to be your best, who like you for who you are, and who remind you what steps to take when you've forgotten the way. They're the ones who always understand what you're going through. They're the people who help you rest assured that your secrets are safe and your hopes are in good hands.

Friends help to balance things out, and they keep you on your toes. They make you smile even when you're stumbling through life, and the stories, support, and laughter they bring to the years feel more like music to your ears than just about anything.

Some friends seem so meant to be. And you are exactly like that for me. We've always just "clicked" and been so connected. And I know we'll stay that way.

You are a beautiful part of the song in my heart and the story of my life. I couldn't ask for a more perfect friend... than you.

— Douglas Pagels

I have always seen my life
as a journey on a road to tomorrow.
There have been hills and valleys
and turns here and there
that have filled my life with
all kinds of challenges and changes.
But I made it through those times,
because there were always
special friends I met along the way.
My special friends are the ones
who have walked beside me,
comforting my spirit or holding my hand
when I needed it the most.
They were friends who loved my smiles
and were not afraid of my tears.
They were true friends
who really cared about me.
Those friends are forever;
they are cherished and loved
more than they'll ever know.

— Deanna Beisser

I Have So Many Wishes for You

I wish you love in your life, hope in your heart, faith in your dreams, and enough encouragement to do whatever would make you happy, keep you healthy, and assure you the prosperity you deserve.

I wish you joy. I wish you peace. I wish you blessings in your life. I wish you answers to questions, resolve to change something that you want to change, and the awareness and ability to accept something that perhaps you haven't been able to change.

I wish you satisfaction in your work and all the other things that would make your day-to-day life more balanced and content and rewarding. I wish you happiness in your family, unconditional love for each other, and understanding. I wish you the capacity and knowledge to embrace the gift of love that dwells in your heart and is replenished when given away.

Everyone is unique and different. I hope you can appreciate your own uniqueness and realize that you're an angel in disguise to some, a friend so important to others, and a member of a family with whom you have significance and importance beyond description.

Special people help us to change our lives, make us feel good about ourselves, and therefore enhance our potential to realize our dreams. They give us a sense of community and belonging. They make us feel appreciated and accepted and move us toward our own emotional security.

If whatever you're wishing for is not covered in these special wishes from my heart to yours, I wish for you your heart's desire because you're so special to me.

— Donna Fargo

You're My
Friend
for Life

When two people have shared
as much as you and I have;
when they've opened up their hearts,
shared their dreams,
thoughts, and fears;
when two people
know each other well enough
to know if sadness
is hiding behind a smile
or if happiness is
glowing in the other's eyes;
when they've shared so many laughs
and when each other's pain
at times has triggered tears;
when two people believe in one another
and are always sincere to each other;
when they have trusted one another
with the truth that lies within —
then you can be sure
that they're friends for life...
just like you and me.

— Zoe Dellous

I Will Carry You
in My Heart
Wherever I May Go

No matter where we go,

we always remember

the wonderful people who touched our lives

and who loved us and helped us

learn more about ourselves.

We always remember

the people who stayed by us

when we had to face difficult times

and with whom we felt safe enough

to reveal our true selves.

Friends are the unforgettable people
we dream and plan
great futures with,
who accept us as we are,
and encourage us to become
all that we want to be.

My friend,
no matter where we go in life
or how far apart we are,
you will always be close to me,
and I will always be your friend.

— Donna Levine-Small

Your Friendship
Is One of
the Nicest Parts
of My Life

If it weren't for you, I wouldn't have half as much laughter or nearly as much joy. I wouldn't have as much peace or understanding. And I definitely wouldn't have as much fun!

I love that you're here. And whether it's in person or on the phone... I love the connection that is always there between us.

What we share is really something special. I feel more at home with you than I do with just about anyone, and feelings like those are some of the most precious of all.

Our friendship will always mean so much to me. It is simply and sweetly the best there is.

— Ann Turrell

Acknowledgments

We gratefully acknowledge the permission granted by the following authors and authors' representatives to reprint poems or excerpts from their publications.

Suzy Toronto for "We Are Kindred Spirits." Copyright © 2011 by Suzy Toronto. All rights reserved.

PrimaDonna Entertainment Corp. for "I Have So Many Wishes for You," "I'll Always Be There for You," "There Is No Stronger Bond Than Friendship," "Some Things Never Change," and "You Are a Real Friend" by Donna Fargo. Copyright © 1999, 2005, 2011, 2012 by PrimaDonna Entertainment Corp. All rights reserved.

Dianne Cogar for "You are appreciated and praised…" and "What I See in You." Copyright © 2012 by Dianne Cogar. All rights reserved.

BJ Gallagher for "Sweet Offering" from A TRUE FRIEND IS SOMEONE JUST LIKE YOU. Copyright © 2007 by BJ Gallagher. All rights reserved.

A careful effort has been made to trace the ownership of selections used in this anthology in order to obtain permission to reprint copyrighted material and give proper credit to the copyright owners. If any error or omission has occurred, it is completely inadvertent, and we would like to make corrections in future editions provided that written notification is made to the publisher:

BLUE MOUNTAIN ARTS, INC., P.O. Box 4549, Boulder, Colorado 80306.